Arachne

POEMS BY AMOS NIVEN WILDER

"Shadows of God, we stretch us shadow-lands;
We spin us ghostly firmaments of gauze
With spirit hands.
Conception bodies forth a realm and draws
Its proper cosmos by its proper laws. . . ."

L'ENVOI

WIPF & STOCK · Eugene, Oregon

Wipf and Stock Publishers
199 W 8th Ave, Suite 3
Eugene, OR 97401

Arachne
Poems by Amos Niven Wilder
By Wilder, Amos N.
Copyright©1928 Wilder Family LLC
ISBN 13: 978-1-4982-1756-9
Publication date 2/27/2015
Previously published by Yale University Press, 1928

TO MY MOTHER

AND THE HOME IN MANSFIELD STREET

SERIES FOREWORD TO THE AMOS N. WILDER LIBRARY

Given the superfluity of books in the world, there has to be a compelling reason to reissue those that have gone out of print. Most often a curious reader can rely successfully on interlibrary loan or Google Books to gain access to what the publishing world has otherwise let drop. But this piecemeal retrieval is not sufficient when an author, rather than a single volume, warrants being brought back into circulation; when there is a whole body of work deserving of a fresh audience. Such is the case with Amos Niven Wilder (1895–1993), whose prodigious writing, spanning the better part of a century, claims our attention with its extraordinary variety of genres (poetry, essay, and memoir) and disciplines (biblical study, literary criticism, theology).

First, the man behind the publications. A gift for writing and a passion for literature were very much in the family's DNA. Named for his newspaper-publisher father, Amos was the eldest of five, four of whom distinguished them as writers. Most famous of them was his only brother, the playwright and novelist Thornton Wilder, about whom he wrote "Thornton Wilder and His

Public" in 1980. Educated at Yale University, from which he eventually received four degrees, he also undertook biblical and theological studies in France and Belgium but most importantly at Mansfield College, Oxford, where he encountered the likes of Albert Schweitzer (*The Quest of the Historical Jesus*) and C.H. Dodd (renown for the notion of "realized eschatology," wherein the end is not near but now). These years of schooling launched his career as a distinguished New Testament scholar at Andover-Newton Theological Seminary, the Chicago Theological Seminary and the University of Chicago, and finally at Harvard Divinity School. Yet perhaps more crucial to his personal development than this academic training was his service in World War I, during which time he served as a volunteer ambulance driver in France and Macedonia (receiving the *Croix de guerre*) and later saw significant action as a corporal with the U.S. Army field artillery in France. That the "Great War" shaped his life and career is suggested by the works that bracket his publications: his first book, a collection of poems, *Battle Retrospect* (1923), and his very last, *Armageddon Revisited: A World War I Journal* (1994). Both bear witness to a traumatic wartime experience that neither destroyed him nor ever let him go.

For many, the trenches marked the end of faith, but not for Wilder. Upon his discharge he went to Yale

Divinity School, was ordained in the Congregational Church, and served briefly as a parish minister in New Hampshire. By the end of the 1920s, however, he was back at Yale to do doctoral work in the New Testament. Impelled by a fascination with eschatology, that branch of theology concerned with "last things," he focused research and imagination on traditional themes: death, the end of the world, and the ultimate destiny of humanity. But this was no antiquarian theological interest; it was his way into a deeper understanding of the Gospel and the times in which he lived. It is not difficult to connect the academic study that culminated in *Eschatology and Ethics in the Teaching of Jesus* (1939, 1950, 1978) with the trauma of World War I; it is even easier to understand why throughout his career he was drawn to the apocalyptic literature of both Jews and Christians. In France he had been inside an apocalypse, had felt the earth reel and rock, had seen the foundations of the world laid bare (2 Sam. 22: 8, 16). It would not do to dismiss these biblical visions, as many did at the time, as surreal and grotesque fantasy; they were, he would argue, grounded in an actual Armageddon he had witnessed firsthand. "Reality" as it had been known before the world had been torn open for judgment. It was time for revelation.

The correspondence Wilder saw between ancient apocalyptic and the experience of his own generation—between notions of biblical crisis and the revolutions of the twentieth century—inspired an already established biblical scholar to become a literary critic as well. Turning to texts sacred and secular, ancient and modern, he discovered in them a common situation, what in a 1971 essay he called "nakedness to Being," an "immediacy to the dynamics of existence." When you live in a ruined world, you must study the ruins. Literature was a place to begin.

He began, in fact, with the particular literature of biblical writers: parable, myth, apocalypse, and Christian rhetoric in all its forms. Moreover, rather than travel the well-worn, dusty paths of the New Testament academy, Wilder invested himself in an exploration of biblical imagination at a time (unlike the present day) when few were doing so. What precisely was the world the Scriptures asked us to enter, and how did language bring it to life? Parable and apocalyptic were especially compelling to him as they emerged, he argued, from "a crucible where the world is made and unmade."

Wilder did not approach the Bible "as literature," but rather as the Word of God articulated in a variety of literary forms. He welcomed the new attention being paid by literary scholars to the Scriptures—Northrop Frye, Robert

Alter, Frank Kermode—and was grateful that windows had been opened "in an ancient library long obscured by stained glass and cobwebs" (as he wrote in an endorsement of Alter and Kermode's *Literary Guide to the Bible*). Yet he was not uncritical of what they found on the sacred page, nor did his interest in literary theory prevent him from arguing against the Deconstructionist notion that biblical narrative (*pace* Kermode's *The Genesis of Secrecy*) was finally indeterminate and open-ended. For Wilder, the Gospel of Mark, for instance, was "too urgent for puzzles and mystification"; it was not a cryptogram but an "opening and crowning disclosure" of glory.

In a daring move for a "guild" scholar, even one long drawn to questions of biblical interpretation, Wilder also opened his readers to the poetry, fiction, and drama of the twentieth century. An early foray into this career-long exploration was *The Spiritual Aspects of Modern Poetry* in 1940; a decade later came the decennial Bross Prize-winning *Modern Poetry and the Christian Tradition* (1952), *Theology and Modern Literature* (1958), and then *The New Voice: Religion, Literature, and Hermeneutics* (1969), where he touches on novelists (Proust, Gide, Sartre) and poets (Eliot, Robert Lowell, David Jones). These books invite the theological reader to be at once nourished and challenged by twentieth-century literature. However, the were written not only to expand the horizons of biblical scholars, but also to develop an interest in religion among those not inclined to seek it out. Still more ambitious is Wilder's 1976 book, *Theopoetic*, with its call for a renewal of biblical religion itself through the cultivation of the imagination. This required the risk of the new, stepping beyond the safety of the familiar and time-worn to explore deeper waters: "Old words do not reach across the new gulfs, and it is only in vision and oracle that we can chart the unknown and new-name the creatures." Before the message, came the vision; before the sermon, the hymn; before the prose, the poem. (He began his life as a writer in 1923, after all, as a Yale Younger Poet.)

Wilder's *The Bible and the Literary Critic*, published in 1991—just two years before his death in his 98th year—offers his own retrospection on a life's work spent on a border between Scripture and literature, proclamation and critique, God's Word and the poet's new account of everything old. Thanks to Wipf & Stock's republication of his works in "The Amos N. Wilder Library," we now have a chance not merely to look back on an extraordinarily varied creative life but to realize anew what it stands to offer our future explorations of the Bible and its literary afterlife.

Peter S. Hawkins
Professor of Religion and Literature
Yale Divinity School
New Haven, CT
October 2013

CONTENTS

INVOCATION

Now would I lull my spirit on the swells of song;
  Balm is there none but beauty for the souls of men,
Nor any poignant solace sterile ways along
Save music, and rhythm, of lyre or voice or pen.

Rhythm is in the winds, and rhythm in the seas,
The heavens chant in numbers, and the springtime and the
        fall
Are pulses in the sagas of the gods, and centuries
Are but the respiration of the eldest Bard of all.

Shall man alone go sullen nor feel the impulse borne
On viewless waves of triumph that surge against his care?
The exultation of great hearts beats at our moods forlorn,
The lift of unheard choruses tugs at our mute despair.

Come then, long rhythms, that pulse beneath the heart,
Come then, slow tremors, that flow about the spheres,
Buoy up our singing on far-borne tides that start
From rolling seas of music out beyond the years.

Leave us not dumb, nor with discordant songs and weak;
We must have music ever lest our hearts grow dull again.
O let us hear once more the dulcet trumpets speak!
Balm is there none but beauty for the souls of men.

WINTER NIGHT

O MAGICAL the winter night! Illusory this stretch
Of unimaginable grays; so shadowy a sketch
Only the fading inks of spirit artistry can etch.

Here is nor dawn nor eventide nor any light we know,
This ghostly incandescence and unearthly afterglow,
This far-spread conflagration of the fields of snow

That pales the clouds, snow-laden, and blanches all the night,
As though in place of moon and stars some spectral satellite
Cast glamor on the earth and floods of violet light.

The wraith-like landscape glimmers, valley, lake and hill,
Unutterably patient! intolerably still!
No inclination of a leaf nor songster's trill.

. . . So could one stand an hour, a day, a century,
Breathless. . . . What frozen silence! What immobility!
As of some gray unfinished world in age-long reverie.

O whither have you vanished, treading the leaves of fall,
Bright spirit of the summer, leaving the scene in thrall
To silence? To what springtime, far, far beyond recall?

What far retreat of being, what ebbing of the flood
Of life to bless far landscapes anew with leaf and bud
Has left this prospect passionless and charmed this stricken
    wood?

. . . And yet from depths how distant, that tide of green
    shall rise,
And that bright spirit come again with April in her eyes,
And winter's pale prostrations be but phantom memories.

2

NOW DREAMS . . .

Now dreams usurp the sway of mortal minds
    And glamors fleet upon the unpeopled earth,
        For all of mortal birth
Morpheus composes and Diana binds.
  The beating sails of thought are furled;
The moon's unruffled ocean floods the world,
And blessed alienation locks the soul
Of dreaming earth in its nocturnal spell;
  Save that that golden overflow
Vainly encroaches on this somber cell:
The deepening Lethe, sanative and slow,
Bathes not this redoubt of unrest and waking,
        Its fever slaking.
Rise to yon mountain heights, you golden stream
        And tide of dream;
Inundate this last citadel of thought.
Submerge, submerge in your slow-breathing trance
        The queries overwrought.
      Nurse the surrendering soul
      With flame from heaven's pole
And lend it, all disarmed, Orion's burnished lance,
        Diana's glance,
The fires of Arcturus, and the Pleiads' flashing dance.

MUGELLO MIDNIGHT

STARS unwatched of man or beast
   Through night's august afternoon,
Soaring slowly from the east
While the world is sunk in swoon,
Sentinels of life, maintain
Life until we live again.

White walls flung athwart the stars,
Rough clay raised to front the night,
Mire transfigured from afar
By their all-investing light,
Sentinels of beauty, keep
Beauty earth-bound while we sleep.

Not the ghostly scepter reared
Richly from some Gothic hall
More unearthly had appeared
Than this chalky Tuscan wall
With its gates and windows charred
By the shades that flood the yard.

Incandescence rained on thought,
Rare effulgence poured on dreams,
Still by man unseen, unsought,
While he lowly plots and schemes,
Hearth of life, thy fires still give
Till man wake at length to live.

Dark souls mined from out the dark,
Lifted up to front the light,
There exposed to God, all stark,
Hallowed in your own despite,

Through the decades may you too
Far-caught splendors so indue.

San Pièro à Sième, Mugello

MENDOTA

I WANDER still in fancy as I wandered long ago
        By Lake Mendota's side,
Resigned at length to memories and absence, satisfied
That even then its loveliness was but a vision, though
I walked barefoot on its pebbles and thought I knew it so.

There as a child I passed bright hours upon the strewn beach
        Intent on stone and shell
And still the wide champaign of light would work in me a
        spell,
And like an incantation was the water's silver speech
Lapsing upon the stones, to charm me out of reach

Of all the waking world; and still in absence even so
        It falls upon my mind:
I see it smoke with luster, and its distant bluffs are lined
With shining bows of fire, while lightenings come and go
Across the liquid firmament where dream sails show.

Its ripples wash upon my dreams for all the years and years
        gone by,
        For all the suns and moons,
Its undulations flood my sleep with light from vanished
        noons;
I still must pore on those quicksilver shallows till I die,
Writhing with magic runes of light beneath a radiant sky.

DAWN IN THE ARGONNE

IF I were blind and could not see
Dawn's slow, stupendous victory,

If I were halt and could not dance
To feel its sweet exuberance,

Or could not sense well, being ill,
The fine pulsation and the thrill,

Or could not smell the incense cold,
So fresh the world cannot be old:

Take sight and smell, take sense and touch,
Leave only (leaving so too much)

The cuckoo's early morning notes
That through the orchard branches float,

Like those low crescent moons at dawn,
Rounded and voyaging, withdrawn;

(Dawn were not dawn were it not heard,
'Twould sing itself were there no bird!)

Still would I seize in that one sign
The dawn, and all its wealth be mine:

A quiet bliss and sense of home
Just out beyond the ways we roam.

April 1917

SUNRISE ON THE HIMALAYAS
FROM TIGER HILL

S NOWS in the night loom in the sullen north
   Beyond an abyss of ridges brimmed with cloud;
Now fade in night's diaphanous eclipse,
And now loom forth
Out of the darkness' fluctuating shroud,
Conscious e'er night has run
Of visitings from the unannouncèd sun.

For these sublime existences ignore
The traffickings of India's darkling floor
And human lore,
And speak each other, beaconing afar
To sun and star
In speech untaught,
And hold a converse far above our thought.
Their language like an undulation leaps
Across heaven's steeps
And laps the headlands of the day and night
With storms of light.

Upon those faces vast,
Invisible beams in night's obscurity
Break into milky radiancy;
There congregate white fires of the past;
The riotous stars have cast
Their silver illustrations on the height
And made the range their glaring satellite.

And like an alien mass
Beyond the confines of our heaving world,
Remote on seas of vapor wide unfurled
As the first shadows pass
And the first pallors of the dawn appear
It floats and overlooks the landscapes of our sphere.

Whiter its chalky facets glow,
Sharper the granite fences show
Under night's paling lamps;
The continental slopes pitch high
Into mid-heaven their jagged ramps,
The lunar cirques and craters lie
Under an irised sky.

Now through the eastern murk the sun
Breaks with his sultry rim
And unto him
Earth tilts its nebulous floor
Till more and more
The auroral couriers run
To lend yon cosmic battlements their crimson benison.

And lucid morning follows in their train;
Day's diamond beam
Like some crystalline inundation brims
The heaven's rims:
The wide inane
Glitters, and bathes the world as in some luminous dream.

The aerial snows indue
A silvery hue;
Metallic glamors fleet upon the slopes.
The spirit gropes

In nameless visions and inhuman tracts
Beyond earth's calms and storms,
The eyeballs seared and blind
With gazing on the eternal cataracts
Of light that pour upon the world of forms
From the exhaustless fountains of eternal mind.

THE TAJ MAHAL

"O Shah Jahan; what a dream!"

A WHITE imagination spun of dream
Hallowed by old mortalities and losses;
Foam of enchantment on the somber stream
Of years with their vicissitudes and crosses;

White lotus on the Sacred River; bud
Blown on the Jumna of the course of man,
To lift his dreams above the weltering flood
And guard them there beyond his little span;

Satellite of the moon, whose lambent glances
Snow its expanding cupolas from far;
Station of light in night's obscure expanses,
And correspondent of each distant star.

All day the velvet-throated cuckoo's lay
Had rung in plenitude of peace around
The cypress precincts, and the perroquet
Had tossed on boughs within the holy ground,

Until the night dissolved the crystal fane
Under the flush of evening to a mist,
An exhalation of immaculate pain,
Of grief and beauty met in ideal tryst.

And now as evening's latest glow is spent
The moonlight blanches domes and lawns and sands,
And o'er the night-charred grove this monument
For the world's tribulation whitely stands:

A meet memorial for the race when we
Have passed, a mausoleum for mankind,
Brightening and darkening ever, silently,
When all our outcries have been left behind;

Focusing all heaven's fires upon its face
Through earth's diurnal revolutions bare;
Witnessing to the tenderness and grace
That lifts above our ravages so rare,

So lovely a memorial, and laves
Our havoc with so ineffable a balm,
Crowns with sidereal flame our sorry graves,
And trances our blasphemings in such calm.

LA FORÊT DE SOIGNES. ROUGE CLOÎTRE

I READ how Ronsard was a lover of woods,
Of his *Gâtine sainte* and its oak brotherhoods:

That Dodonian grove with its dim abodes
That he named the mother of demi-gods,

With its swaying chambers of beech and oak
That he called the high house of the leafage folk;

Of its sacrosanct depths in far away vales
And the Pans at play in its charmed pales.

And I thought of the woods by Fiesole
And the phantom ladies that thither flee,

And the cavaliers, from the plague of the town,
Discoursing, and pacing up and down.

And I thought of a night above Grasmere,
How I slept in the woods with the waters near

And woke in the hush of the early dawn
To see the dusk from the lake withdrawn,

Gleaming between the silent trees
With a message from all the eternities.

But most I thought of a sacred hill
Whose autumnal precincts waver still

In memory, with its dazzling floor
Smoldering for evermore.

A lambent flame plays over the leaves,
An unnatural color the eye deceives;

13

A dread comes on the soul to grope
About that incandescent slope.

Ever it takes me by surprise
And my thoughts will straightway volatilize,

However sunken, when into view
In autumn comes that avenue

On avenue of pillar'd beeches
Stretching away in endless reaches,

Lifting to heaven like purple shades
From the flaming soil in far colonnades,

Blue exhalations pendent there
From the sacred earth in the sacred air,

A spiritual grove from a spiritual soil
Beyond man's power to despoil,

In which one wanders like a ghost,
Soundlessly, and all engrossed

In groves and tracks of phantasy
Coursed dizzily and buoyantly;

A world outside, a world apart,
A solace for a fevered heart,

An apparition lent an hour
As earnest of the eternal dower,

A glimpse of the new firmaments
That lie beyond the world of sense.

CLOUD ARGOSIES

THERE is that in me paints the clouds with flame:
      Some leaping fire
   Of joys without a name;
    Some blazing pyre
   That through my eyes
Casts on the outer spectacle
  Its ruddy light and dyes
Heaven's cloud-banked panorama with its hues,
Tingeing yon conclave down the remotest skies.

There is that in me sets the heavens afire:
      Some kindling hope,
   Some uncontained desire,
Flaming within me like a stormy dawn
Lays out its orient banners o'er the earth
Till heaven from horizon unto cope
   Is one great conflagration.
Hope's mad incendiary rushes on
Scaling the heights with a delirious mirth,
   Till by his roaring torch
The bluest pastures of the aether smoke and scorch.

    .   .   .   .   .

They sleep in endless series in the vault,
The azure vault of the cerulean air,
Like snowy frigates when the time is fair
And summer's lightest breezes make default;
   Moored on that glassy sea
In long processional they stretch away
Down the remotest flood-tides of the day
   In immobility;

Their full-blown sails aetherial, rose and blond,
      The fabulous wrack,
Streaming along its greater ocean track,
Vanishes down the roads of the beyond.

A prodigy! From heavens rich in balm,
Or from some continent where nature smiles
Beyond the poles, or from the Blessed Isles,
Or from some mart where souls are wise and calm,
Trading in dreams and seeking love's increase,
      This argosy of peace!
Over unnumbered leagues of silence borne
The thousand-oared Armada of the clouds,
Freighted with beauty, sets, with all its shrouds
Peopled with visitants, toward earth's dark bourne.

Ho! ye who thirst for beauty and for dreams,
Parched for that heaven's streams have ceased to flow,
Famished for that earth's treasure has run low,
You unto whom the tide of beauty seems
Long to have ebbed from life's now sterile sands,
Each year to leave its iron coasts more bare,
Each year more grudgingly its dews to spare
      To heights and meadow-lands.

Come ye who labored for a sign too rare,
Come ye who hoped the miracle too long,
Who found no manna desert ways along,
And won of rapture all too small a share,
Nor saw the angel 'mid the crippled throng
Trouble the waters by the Bethesdan stair.

Come ye who stooped to touch last autumn's leaves
As earth's last trace of glory, and in mourning
Frequent the winter woods where nature grieves
Beauty's demise, and doubt spring's new adorning.

Come ye whom beauty's farthing overwhelms;
Lo, here is ransom for a thousand hosts.
Some rich consignment sped toward other realms
Lights by some hazard on our nether coasts.
Yon dazzling fleet from alien oceans strayed,
Freighted with balm and incense for some race
Of holier beings, by our shores delayed,
Along earth's wharves its shipment will unlade,
Its cargoes fabulous of awe and grace.

O miracle of grace, joy, tears of joy,
            O blessed sign;
Too sweet, too near, too great for worth of mine.
After eternities of barren care
            The eventual fruit of prayer.
            After the pain
            And thirst and dark annoy
Excessive grace dissolves the heart again.
O miracle of grace, joy, tears of joy.

VISIONS BY THE LAKE OF ORTA

L ET not harsh tongues do violence to this spell,
    Nor futile speech nor rhythms feebly borne,
        Nor song forlorn;
Music alone hath language in this dell,
And numbers like the tremors of a bell
        That swell and swell
Accordant with the tenor of the rhythmic morn.

        Against its crystal walls
        Our frustrate language falls;
Here needeth some diviner eloquence,
Some grammar won from angels and some word
Richer and ampler than we yet have heard,
        And some diviner sense.

If beauty be the element of song,
Itself a frozen music and a choir
Inaudible, so let me be the lyre
        To give thee voice
And to the world thine oracles prolong;
Bid thine inanimate praise in vocal song rejoice.

I

FROM THE SACRO MONTE

Like some quicksilver overflow, or some
Blue writhing serpent serpentinely sprawled
Along the vale, whose mailed limbs glisten from

The triumphant sun, in molten beauty thralled,
See Cusio's lustrous firmament outspread,
Sparkling with lightenings and Alpine-walled,

Cusio: *The name of this Piedmontese lake in the time of the ancients.*

18

With deep subaqueous springs pellucid fed
To take its every color from the skies
And render every tremulous image shed

On its invisible breast, and sympathize
With all its blue environing majesties.

Like some mirage of brighter atmospheres,
Richer champaigns and more translucent seas,
Somnolent isles in calm and radiant meres,

Like some mirage that we a moment seize,
Canvased in brilliance on our desert haze,
Displaced from distant climes by mysteries

Of cloud and heat, whereby we briefly gaze
On chases unpermitted and on shows
Forbidden, sacred and beyond our ways,

So liest thou in apparition that grows
More vivid momently and glows and glows,

Speaking of some lost world beyond the world,
Speaking of some lost sea beyond the sea,
Speaking of some remembered wave that purled

Upon a brighter strand perennially,
Of towers round which no ghostly clamors ring
And lives whose rounds are set to harmony,

Of hearts that cast the memory of the sting
And harrying of this world's delirium,
Pacing the cloisters of eternal spring

With buoyant sense, their fortunes overcome,
Tasting the fruit of mortal martyrdom.

Here let despondency at length take heart
And here let long remorse itself grow mild.
Where such unearthly apparitions start,

Such shadowings on the Alpine reaches wild,
Such bright communications by the brink,
Where songs of unseen spirits reconciled

Re-echo, and where mortal eyes must shrink
And love so flame upon us from the earth,
Upon the words of *Beatrice* think:

A growing splendor where the soul knew dearth
Augurs the clearer sight and heavenly birth.

2

FROM THE TORRE DI BUCCIONE

Here let imagination take its fill,
That inner Muse that gazes through our eyes
But keepeth counsel till it be her will
To give it utterance and make us wise.
Pore on this tranquil lake, this shadow-land
Of slumbering Alps, this shadow-dragging wrack,
These hamlets glassed in beauty where they stand
Or in the massy waters mirrored back.
Pore on this quiet island from the flood
As though within the very instant risen,
Its ancient tower and walls, its cypress wood,
Rising in magic from its watery prison:

An isle of Paradise upon the wave
Of dreams, reflected from beyond the grave.

Here let imagination take its fill
And capture these enigmas to its use,
Sup on these forms and figures as it will
And read where wit and fancy plead excuse.
The transformations of the patterned lake
To least impress of heat and light and wind
Betray how sensitive the earth did wake
Beneath the touch of the creating mind.
Range upon range beyond our blunt remark
These holier servants of the deity,
Rain, wind and waters, color, light and dark,
Meet in divine exchanges endlessly:
A symphony of symphonies to teach
The intelligent soul by an exquisite speech.

With deeper blue the lake is overcast,
The snows drive down their chargers noiselessly,
The heavens foam above, a shade has passed,
Ultramarine, upon the lacquered sea.
The ranging notes of belfries ride the wind,
The charmèd island speaks the charmèd tower,
And medieval voices still will find
A medieval answer to this hour.
Eyes gaze on many a resplendent sight,
Ears savor many an harmonious tone,
Alone imagination reads by right
And hears the language of the ages gone:
To her each deepening hue, each tolling bell,
Speaks intimations that no tongue can tell.

FROM THE TERRACE OF THE MADONNA DELLA BACCIOLA

Here as I trod your hills, withheld, debarred,
And looked upon your lineaments in despair,
Finding them incommunicative, hard,
All unaware

I passed into the landscapes of the soul
And saw your waters in the mind of God;
Nor form nor hue but served the harmonious whole,
Nor leaf nor clod.

Divine imagination ruled the scene:
The transcendent artist, master of all form,
Had woven together on the mountain screen
The glooms of storm:

Color and shape and sound, odor and sense,
An infinitude of elements combined,
And, miracle of miracles, intense
With change, yet change to harmony assigned.

I stood and watched the eternal dreamer work,
Traced his creative act from hour to hour,
Whose canvases no rebel mediums irk,
Whose dawning thoughts upon the instant flower.

I saw the Alpine bastions ebb and flow,
And these so solid-seeming hills in rain
And sunlight, mist and glare, now gloom, now glow,
Melt and dissolve, reform and shape again.

Calmness grown visible, the balm of sight,
The element's self of sheer tranquillity,
The burnished mere—a filigree of light—
Raveled its shining hems perennially.

The toil of man himself was effortless
And full of silent music in that hour;
He moved as constellations, without stress,
He moved as conquerors in their day of power.

There far beneath me on the molten lake
I saw the boatman's bright oars palpitate;
I know not if I slept or was awake
So perfect every trait;

And there that century-sombered tower below
Upon the oblivious isle that heeds no whit
Our coming and our going, nor doth know
Of us nor of these days that wash on it,

Unless by that same mood we enter in
Its medieval reverie, or grown
Contemporaries of the hills thus win
Their moment for our own. . . .

4

FROM THE SAME

New illustrations flame upon this glass
Of nature's mind, new breathings and new jets:
These forms are beings, and their modes surpass

Our scope; though when the snowy cloud woof frets
The blue, or April's waxy leafage blows,
Or when the incendiary sun-god sets,

Or when with thousand fires the water flows
Or platinum-blue beneath an inky sky,
We feel they are alive and do unclose

To the dread organ of the Phantasy
Intelligible language, wordlessly.

Orta Novarese, 1923

ANNALS OF CIRCUMSTANCE AND BEAUTY

SONNETS

Alas! the endowment of immortal power
Is matched unequally with custom, time,
And domineering faculties of sense. . . .

The Excursion

Dust as we are, the immortal spirit grows
Like harmony in music; there is a dark
Inscrutable workmanship that reconciles
Discordant elements. . . .

The Prelude

FLOW back, flow back upon the amazèd soul,
    Flood of divine remembrance! From your sleep
Where vanished moons their spectral sessions keep,
O vanished hours, rise to our day! Unroll,
Unroll once more the illuminated scroll
Of memory's golden legend from the deep
And bid its glowing evocations sweep
Athwart the night of thought from pole to pole.
So shall we learn what losses have been ours
And count how many deaths the living die,
Note the divorce of souls for aye and aye
That, joined, had triumphed o'er the victorious hours,
And mourning these lost loves and broken faiths
Know all for shadows and ourselves for wraiths.

Evocation

WE pass through worlds and worlds in sleep;
    The pilgrim in the lowly inn
Bears no trace of the mighty deep
Nor of the spheres where he has been.
We pass through Limbos, and forget;
Impoverished of our shadowy lore
Of principalities that yet
Glimmer, and powers we sense no more.
For no substantial being is ours.
We glass the deep abysses blind,
And there the flare of Tophet lowers
Where late the Seven Candles shined.
We traverse suns and moons in sleep
And guard no records of the deep.

*Transmigration
and amnesia*

THE flagellations of the world have made
Me mild and sad; I care no more for strife.
On going This sphere admits not of that clearer life
into slavery Art mirrors; for the curse will be obeyed,
And on the soul the grieving yoke is laid:
Sin, and the indignities of bread and roof,
And, lest the heart aspire too far, aloof,
Society's cruel hold none may evade.
Relinquish the ecstatic dream, renounce
Communion with the dawn, the earth, the dead;
Sore-hearted lift the moment's temporal load,
And when the darkening prospects soon announce
The end of freedom and the vision sped,
Scorn the pretense of courage on that road.

BEAUTY prepares while lingering moons revolve.
Her gradual hosts foregather on many strands,
But not for us! O not for us! Dissolve
In tears, Endymion, and wring white hands,
Frustration You daughters of desire, alas, alas.
But not for us. The silver beacons catch;
We see the kindled tale of triumph pass
To peaks that past our dark horizons stretch.
Alas, O Follower, alas, alas,
You shall not know that City's ecstasy,
Its throngs' seraphic murmur. Glories mass
And gestate over continent and sea,
But not for us who reach our hands and pass,
The Unpermitted, O alas, alas.

I T is not I who wrestle in these toils
  Of custom and occasion, O not I,
Not I, so scored and lacerated by
The day's indignities whose hurt despoils
The soul of its dominion and soils
With reek and blood its native majesty,
And 'tis not I whose high serenity
Contumely stings, humiliation foils.
That is not I, or then if I it be,
How other from myself that view in trance
The eternal hour's immobility!
Froz'n in still beauty's moment that advance
Or passing knows not, but perennially
Shines, to annul outrageous circumstance.

*Circumstance
and beauty*

W E live forever who one moment live
   In beauty's seizure; we may not go free.
Caught for all time in that captivity
The summoned spirit like a sphere doth give
Its reins to its compelling sun, and drive
In everlasting rounds, obediently,
Seized in her orbit and her harmony,
Forever driven, singing, and alive.
It is a dream that we should seem to toil
And suffer and rebel and faint and sin,
Bruised and tormented in this mortal coil;
No, no, our spirits are beyond this din
And there where hurtless fires all strifes assoil
Through long cerulean revolutions spin.

*The eternal
hour*

It is not that we rhyme for coin or praise,
    We starvelings at the Fair of flesh and wit,
We fools of ribald courts whose heaven-snatched phrase
The troubadour Is tossed from mocking stage to jeering pit;
    It is not for the fireside or the crust,
    Nor for the flattery of cajoling cheats,
    Nor to be in men's thoughts when we are dust
    That we cry staves in the contemptuous streets,—
    Like madmen, held in awe and spit upon,
    Loathed for our pain, we rave of peace and heaven,
    Tortured by angels, staggering and wan
    And wretched, by two worlds disputed, riven,—
    Only we would some fellow gleeman find
    Within these hells and Edens of the mind.

I own I have been startled into fear
    To see upon some dark December night
The stricken fields and slopes grow strangely bright
Winter moonrise And faery shadows silently appear,
    And at that melancholy time of year
    When only stubble shows and earth is cold,
    To see the landscape filled with waving gold
    And sudden harvests gleam where all was sere;
    Yet must I think it stranger still to find
    How when the heart is at its winter time
    Of barrenness and drear sterility,
    Such glimpses raise a harvest suddenly
    Of golden sentiments, whence skylarks climb,
    In the illumined landscapes of the mind.

ETHEREALIZE once more, you brazen house,
Congealed and shrunken tenement of dust,
You leaden earth, O blank and sterile crust,
Again from your soul-drowning slumber rouse;
Flicker with emerald flames, you torpid boughs,
Once more, and you dark crowded heavens, thrust
Awful insurgencies with each new gust
Above that earth your phantom pageant cows.
Dissolve, enkindle, smoke, and vaporize,
Too heavy scene! O once mysterious earth,
Once more appear to our appallèd eyes
That dreadful theater wherein the birth
And death and old atonements of the race
Fit celebration find in nature's face.

*Summons to
nature*

*to reflect
the human
drama.*

INCUMBENT splendors march and countermarch
Upon the cliffs of heaven; the sea of light
Is coursed by squalls of shadow that affright
The earth; and burnished suns inflame the arch
Of day, or blanchèd moons their milky haze
Silt through the spaces of the Indian vault;
The august-sessioned seasons seems to halt
In plenitude, and time's old ravage stays.
Above our heads the dread procedure runs;
Heaven shifts its awful scenes in wrack and storm.
Sublime transactions toward, its sympathies
Stretch curtains to empanoply the frieze
Of earth with sable shrouds, or now reform
The azure walls about earth's denizens—

*Nature's august
procedure,*

*sympathizing
with man,*

B UT we, while all the synod of the steep
Gleam through their shining offices serene,
and man's Under their vagrant lightnings still demean
indignity. Our courses to the lampless ways that creep
Through damps and vapors to the second sleep
That fondles us with its embrace obscene,
Beckoning the frustrate soul (the while convene,
Above, those heralds) to the starless deep.
Cry to "the Angels and couriers of the plains of light!
shining synod You extricated souls, recalling sin,
of the blest" But lapped in flames of love against relapse,
Plunge from that high consistory in flight
To snatch us to your refuge, so to win
The immunity that zone and star enwraps!

N OT clamorously shouting in the woods
With noisy revellers that know thee not,
Nor seeking reverie in this cloistral spot
And suave responses and thy sylvan moods,
Nor only in thy spiritual goods
To share, O Nature, and with peace to blot
The turbulence with which our days are fraught
Anaemia Seek I this haven where no ill intrudes;
But with far deeper hunger and a far
More earnest supplication here full-length
I fling myself upon the living sod,
Asking no less than that thy giant strength
Reclaim me to the life in tree and star
By blood transfusion from the veins of God.

O LYRIC Insight, O clairvoyant gaze,
　O flash of lightning from the eternal cope
That lends the veiled imagination scope
And occult vistas to the mind displays;
O long withheld anointing, why delays
The vision, as in garish ways we grope,
Starved of the hidden manna, faint to hope,
And wooed to blindness by the ungenial days.
O that again as in the days gone by,
Blessed with the true illusions of the heart,
Light-headed in the city streets, alarmed
With portents, gorged with visions, head held high,
We might again pass through the sordid mart,
The tawdry shops, the sensual throng, unharmed.

Invocation

B ESTRIDDEN by the god and vexed to read
　The dread foreshadowings of the strifes to be,
The Sibyl in prophetic agony
Knew no such rage as mine, nor extreme need
Of blessed utterance, nor to be freed
From such a weight and press of mystery,
Such rending talons of fell poignancy,
As when I heard your Promethean voices plead;
O Chopin, stormer of the gates of ruth,
Extortioner of tears, importunate
Of pity, who in exultation dost sweep,
And pathos, to invest the holds of truth,
To trumpet down the adamant of fate,
And coerce mercy from the unanswering deep.

*Apollo and
the Sibyl*

Chopin

To create beauty in so dark a world!
And sing out of rejection and despair—
The bird astray in Hades whose song purled
The bird that There in the lava and the lifeless air—
sang in Hell Pitiful and sublime, in the deep murk,
This nether world without its sun or star,
Where cries resound and evil spirits lurk,
Here where the king of terrors is not far;
Something divine, here in so dark a place,
And blessed, to achieve a perfect act,
To lift such challenge to the realms of grace
From realms with torment and with darkness wracked:
In exile and estrangement, all forlorn,
To lift and blow Childe Roland's dauntless horn.

God loves the shabby hero and forlorn,
Sainthood in rags, and courage without means,
Grace in disgrace, royalty stable-born,
And history disguised in common scenes;
Grace in God loves humiliation and reproach
disgrace Since Christ made every ignominy dear,
And Cinderella in her golden coach
Is not so graced as in her lowlier sphere.
God loves the poor man's riches ridiculed,
The flower in the tenement, the marred
And all pathetic gesture overruled,
The offering checked, the eagerness debarred;
God loves the furred hepatica that blows
Credulous in the latter winter snows.

I saw a miracle beside the path:
An apple tree in its first blossoming,
Absurdly small to lift against the wrath
Of Alpine brewings such a show, and fling
A spray, a snow, a burst, an incandescence,
A white éclosion like an angel's wing
Into this unknown scene; an iridescence
Of playing fires, the soul of the new-born,
Rioting in the open in the presence
Of Monta Rosa's menace; from some bourne
Of holy, fragile, jeweled, cherished things,
Unwarned, unapprehending, mid the scorn
And bludgeons of the hail-storm; how it brings
Rebuke of faith to our world's underlings.

Miracle by the
Sacro Monte
of Orta

From fevered crawlings o'er Siberian tracts,
Rushes and faintings on the boundless steppes,
To issue on the silvered cataracts
Of the Pacific and direct one's steps
Along its moonlit gulfs and promontories
And overlook its dazzling pools; from blind
Phantastic toilings round the spiral storeys
Of hell's inverted cone to emerge and find
The stars again; from traffics to and fro
And shuttle ferryings within the mole
To thread some Indian archipelago,
Some endless Thousand Islands of the soul:
So was it at thy touch from my deep vein
Of dark conceits to glimpse the world again.

Convalescence

T HOU art engraven in the bronze of thought.
  Thy face is stamped above the swirl of time.

Pierre de Thou liv'st forever and forever, wrought
Ronsard to At love's high noon, arrested at thy prime.
Cassandre They are not all whose momentary flush
Of beauty on the adamant is limned,
Whose dead eyes burn, whose ashen cheeks still blush,
Alone of time's wronged fresco-hosts undimmed.
The million beings writhe like fumes of smoke
Beneath the dying suns on dying spheres,
And systems topple like the toppling oak,
Oblivion muffles the forgotten years;
But thou shalt time's vast overthrows elude
And smile in thought's immune beatitude.

T HE scythes of time play havoc with the swarms
  That breed and sicken on our dying globe

Shakespeare And shadowy harvests of unnumbered forms
to the friend Fall to the ruthless shafts that search and probe;
of the Sonnets The circling moons put in their silvery flail,
Earth's gibbering phantoms flutter to the shade;
At last the moon's own lustrous course shall fail
And cinders strew the track the Pleiads made.
But thy dream-molded face shall haunt the gods
Embalmed in pity in the eternal thought,
And leap oblivion in those high abodes
To live anew in Edens newly wrought.
Then from this closing dark, O lighted face,
Bear record of me to that shining place.

ACROSS the lost horizons of the years
    I hear sometimes the desultory guns
Trampling the midnight with a throb that runs
From ancient wars to strike upon our ears,   *The eventual*
Baying across the moonlit hemispheres   *peace*
Of dreams to bruit its thunders to the sons
Of days to be amid their benisons
Of towers inviolate by unmenaced meres.
No, no, the jar of sacrilegious war
Shall never shock that crystal atmosphere
Nor roll its angry surf upon that shore
With trepidation and the primal fear,
But till the moon in heaven be no more
Abundant peace shall lock the magic sphere.

LOVE dreamed this place, it was not made by time;
    Glistening forever in its firmament
Of pure transparency—a glow unspent
Poured from the imagination in the prime   *The Tomb of*
And ecstasy of its conceit sublime;   *Ezra, on the*
Love dreamed these mirrored domes and palms, love blent   *Tigris River*
These hues and forms in its own element
Of floating glamour and its crystal clime.
It hangs there like some prospect of the soul,
Vanishing and abiding, as the arc
Of heaven glows upon some drifting mist.
O magic passion whose serene control
So luminously shaped the formless dark
To leave us record of thine ancient tryst.

THE signature of mind is on the deep
  And thought has sunk its seal upon the inane,
And sudden fancies made incursion on sleep,

Logos And flashes lightened o'er the night's domain.
Eternity shall hold the print of dreams;
Their subtle webs and filaments shall lie
Frozen in breathless climates in the seams
Of nature like some lost fern's gossamer die.
Form in the adamantine bastions, form!
Form in the crystal sphere, the triple bronze,
Form out of naught, to outlive with type and norm
Time's crawling insect-hill that slaves and spawns.
The soul is stamped on some Atlantian range
And silence chambers it above all change.

THE VISION OF PURGATORY

To Florence Earle Coates

1

THE fine excitements of the soul, the mood
   Of poetry wherein high dreams are blown
In gay luxuriance and multitude,

When sweet insanity is on the throne
And mused enchantment makes the world its thrall;
These seizures, once the moment's sway be flown,

How mad appear and high-fantastical!
Constructions of a brief delirium,
Evanishing and fictive, morbid all—

A fever at whose fire the veins will drum
And smoky visions earth's clear aspect blur
With false foreshadowings of the world to come;

Spells woven of such silken gossamer
They are not when they touch day's fretful stir.

2

These freaks of insight, openings of thought,
And evanescent colorings and shapes,
And in the stupored spirit, high-distraught,

Sense of emancipations and escapes,
Mergings of unknown powers from the deeps
Of reverie with nature's known landscapes;

How shall we hold them? Or as one who steeps
His soul in fumes and casts the illusion off?
Or one who drinks of Helicon, and weeps,

And calls the world the dream, content to doff
The fashion of the age, and to the spring
Again and yet again return to quaff

Imagination's fury, following
The trance of beauty though it stab and sting?

3

Here blown upon such breath of phantasy
I walked and knew it for another place,
Swoll'n with some wild intoxicant of glee

I knew myself as of another race,
Buoyed on some high conceit that opened wide
The bronze doors of the local commonplace.

Sorrow and glee were walking by my side;
Their counsel bred clairvoyance and surmise;
And all the dead that in our spirits hide

Gazed on this very prospect with my eyes:
The dead that rise forever in our hearts
To feed our life with their lost memories,

To nourish sense with their clandestine arts
And play in us anew their finished parts.

4

My prospect grew a prospect of their world,
These pines with their eternal forests merged,
Around the isle their timeless waters curled;

Our skies with their enkindled masses surged;
My sorrow was the sorrow of a host
And in their company my sin was purged.

I walked with Dante on a nether coast
Beneath unsullied heavens in the gloom
Of snowy birches and great pines, engrossed

In contemplation there beyond the tomb,
Amazed to know that time and space are naught,
Nor all the dreaded barriers that loom

For mortals, since the world so burden-fraught
A world of spirits is and spirit-wrought.

5

I learned how hope could conquer circumstance
And vault the phantom barriers of time,
I learned to mock the incidence of chance

And wait each true conjunction at its prime.
Marmoreal friezes walled the arch of heaven,
Cornelian cloudings stained the wrack sublime,

And through the somber western copses driven
The fires of sunset pierced that nether grove
Where loitering spirits, chastened and new shriven,

Won absolution by a lake of love,
(Whose waters ranged about that twilight isle
Glassing its swaying birches by each cove)

And after purgatorial pains and trial
Took convalescence in that dim asyle.

Birch Island,
Upper St. Regis Lake, N. Y.
1923.

TEN YEARS AGO, MARCH 21, 1918

The 17th Field Artillery, 2d Division.

TEN years ago our column crossed the Meuse—
And I record it lest none other does:

Detrained, and billeted a night or two
Behind Verdun (Verdun! and we were new),

We mounted at the dusk and took our march
Behind the guns, the twenty-first of March.

The moon was bright, the night was still—and there
The Hills of Death with their sepulchral stare.

Somnolent, ominous, with now a blunt
Report that told no tales, we sensed the Front.

The Front, that Ultima Thule, whose ultimate rod
The millions guarded as the frontier of God;

The Front, that fatal River, by whose verge
Millions wrought, frantic lest the world submerge.

Our guns and caissons thundered on the bridge,
No lightning answered from the Woëvre ridge.

The Meuse amid its sedges dreamed too deep
In moonlight to be startled from its sleep.

Its gilded waters had their life too far
In ancient nature to remark our war.

Our echoes died upon the loosened timbers,
We climbed the Right Bank with our heavy limbers,

And passed in clamor, under the Great Wain,
One of the calcined Cities of the Plain.

We left the river and we left the marsh
And felt the grade that leads to Les Éparges.

The night was still, a desultory thunder
Far in the west hardly aroused our wonder.

But then an undertone grew to a hum,
We heard the Allied bombing squadrons come.

The hum grew to a mighty pulse, and soon
The midnight was a-throb beneath the moon.

The deafening revolutions stunned our ears
As though we heard the gyrations of the spheres.

The moon was bright; we saw their silhouettes
Pass o'er its face upon their way to Metz:

The insects floated o'er the argent disk
Ten thousand miles from earth—beyond all risk,

Safe in the world of myth, and led us too
Into the apotheosis that they knew.

For silence fell upon the toiling line,
The shadowy convoy recognized the Sign.

A stupor seized the long nocturnal train,
Guide, staff, interpreter alike drew rein.

Driver and cannoneer gestured above,
Almost the regiment forgot to move.

Across the zenith passed the Icarian throng,
The whole concave of heaven rang like a gong.

Castor and Pollux at Lake Regulus!
But Prodigy had likewise greeted us

And we went into battle under omens
Like all before, Trojans and Greeks and Romans,

And like Achilles we went in the bolder
To know the gods were fighting at our shoulder.

Time was no more, the veils of earth were riven
As we went on into the Wars in Heaven,

And we drew forward over ground we knew,
Megiddo, Marathon and Waterloo,

Saw phalanxes and cohorts wheel like mists
And knew ourselves within the eternal lists.

ARMAGEDDON. *Forêt de Villers-Cotterets, July 18, 1918*

The crux and turning-point of the World War is usually assigned to the dawn of July 18, 1918. At that time, after a feverish mobilization in the great woods near Soissons of Highlander, Moroccan, and other units, including the first and second American divisions, General Mangin, under Marshal Foch's orders, attacked eastward, threatening the German Marne salient. The desperate rush to the front in the great beech forests during that rainy night and the attack at 4.25 remain one of the outstanding epic actions of the war. The overtones of the event and its portentous significance were obscurely felt by those who took part in it.

WAS it a dream that all one summer night
We toiled obscurely through a mighty wood
Teeming with desperate armies; toiled to smite
At dawn upon the unsuspecting height
Above, the Powers of Darkness where they stood?
Was it a dream? Our hosts poured like a flood

In ceaseless cataract of shadowy forms
Along the dark torrential avenues.
Within, the host unseen, unseeing, swarms;
Without, the blind foe's nervous shell-fire storms,
And groping plane its flares, suspicious, strews
Above the cross-roads where the columns fuse.

Dwarfed in the enormous beeches and submerged
In double night we labored up the aisles
As in an underworld; our convoys surged
Like streams in flood, and now our torrents merged
With other torrents from the blind defiles
As hurrying units joined our crowded files.

The hoarse confusion of that precipitate march,
The night-long roar that hung about that train,
Lost itself in the branches that o'erarch
Those passages, and to the heaven's far porch
No whisper rose, but all that agonized strain
Of myriads clamored to the skies in vain.

Beneath a load of palpable dark we bowed.
Smothered in hours with time itself we strove.
The wilderness stood o'er us like a cloud
Opaque to bar bright futures disallowed,
Denying dawn, as though the vindictive grove
Eternal night around our legions wove.

Was it a dream, that rush through night to day?
Far in the depths of night we labored on,
Out of the core of midnight made our way
To meet the grandiose daybreak far away,
While unknown thousands brushed us and were gone,
Whence, whither, in that night's oblivion.

Oaths, shouts and cries rose o'er the incessant din
Of wheel and hoof, and many a frantic blow.
The dazed beasts battle through that tumult in
The darkness at the driver's lash to win
A goal unknown; nor do the thousands know
The event in course, but likewise blindly go.

The deed was too stupendous for our days:
The hopes of millions centered on our act.
We toiled beneath the concentrated gaze
Of quick and dead. Man's quest seemed at the phase
Of consummation; the atmosphere was wracked
With signs that ancient dream grew present fact.

That night we knew the pains of all who fought
And died before they saw the vantage won.
That night we bore the cross of all who wrought
And died before they reached the goal they sought.
That night we travailed with the martyrs gone;
The martyrs triumphed with us at the dawn.

That night we paced the centuries of pain,
That night reviewed the scaffold and the pyre,
Revisited the torments of the slain,
And kept the amazèd vigil once again
Of Him who as the deathly shade drew nigher
Saw the last lights in height and depth expire.

That night we groped with bleeding feet the way,
That night with lacerated flesh the path,
With fiery brain, the age-long road that lay
Between old chaos and the refulgent day;
A thousand thousand years, that night of wrath
We trod again creation's ancient swath.

That night we joined the ancient souls in pain,
That night we toiled up the degrees of hell;
Released by an excess of mortal strain
The immortal world of souls we could regain:
Live in an hour, by torment's timeless spell,
The aeonian discipline and therein dwell.

The face of nature dissipates and blows
Like shredding mists; the mountains and the seas
With groves and fields and cities and the shows
Of time and place grow shadowy, and the throes
Within the soul of man dissolve all these
And conjure up the soul's eternities,

Wherein as in a spiritual realm
We move as ghosts amid a myriad throng
Whose viewless passions our dim wills o'erwhelm
To sweep us on their ecstasies to whelm
The ranks of Ill, the Satanic powers, the strong
Dark adversaries and redoubts of wrong.

The world about us fluid ebbs and flows.
An awful sea of darkness dims the earth.
Nature is other, and its seeming grows
Portentous and chimerical. There glows
An incandescence from some auroral hearth.
Winds blow that sweep not from the planet's girth.

Through midnight's sullen port and leaden gate
We stumble out upon the lists of God.
Diverging from the highways of this state
We lose ourselves within a forest great,
Pass through a mountain, issue on a sod
Man has ignored but which the dead have trod.

There grows the dawn upon a table-land
Feverish with the divine act and last campaign.
The great transaction swells; the myriads stand
Wrought to a pitch of expectation, and band
On band of envoys scour the electric plain,
And squadrons clash on the aerial main.

The angelic signal now the day-spring hails
And pandemonium shakes the awakened earth.
The unseen artillery in groves and vales
Punctures the taut air with its silver nails;
The elastic hammers beat in Jovian mirth
And drive their droning couriers singing forth.

To die was naught; we companied with the dead.
They died who came back to this blinder life.
We lived in death, and those who fell were led
All unaware to battle on instead
With new reliefs in the same field of strife
And passed without a hint from life to life.

They died who came back to this blinder scene
And woke to know the solar year again,
Nor know the pit of souls and vast demesne
Of wars in heaven, but once again demean
Their lives to briefer cycles and contain
Their souls to briefer rounds and common pain. . . .

ELEGY IN THE BETHLEHEM CHAPEL AND ARLINGTON NATIONAL CEMETERY

In Memory of Woodrow Wilson

From these appalling silences the dead
    Attend our tread.
  We drag our living cross
Of consternation and exquisite loss
Through their marmoreal quiets and their wards
    Assuaged and hallowèd,
Sealed with august immunity and calm accords.

Our long delirium, their awed repose;
Our alienation and infirmity,
Our crucifixion, and their reverie
That weaves a silence o'er forgotten foes
And falls on us like some benign orchestral close.

    His fate is dark to us,
    His lot mysterious;
Such destinies are wrought out on a plane
    We probe in vain.
    The human frailty,
    The stress and strain,
The exaltation, strife, and contumely,
And contradiction, and the mortal chain
Of lethargies and humors and delights—
    Our days and nights—
All these do but conceal some perfect rôle,
    Some logic in the whole.
These human moments when he strove and fell
  Were but the mask and the disguise
Of some completed drama in the soul,
Some common lot with those he led, some sacrifice
    Whose end the gods know well.

So is it here on earth:
We serve transcendent ends
Blindly; our deed transcends
These shows and brings to birth
Effects beyond our dearth.

So is it among men:
Our iron circumstance,
Weakness, and the advance
Of hours that bring again
Frustration and mischance;

And yet these strivings blind,
This travail and this pain,
Are tissue of some brain,
The cell-work of a Mind
That waxes as we wane.

Our blind toils are the cells
That build a higher being
To see beyond our seeing,
And in our tedium dwells
A virtue for our freeing.

So in the ambiguous texture of his days
A Reason dwelt whereof we can but dream.
        Things are not what they seem.
The soul of history escapes our gaze.
But in the vision of eternity,
        If we could see,
His life lies interwoven with the dead,
        With those he led;
        His lot
Inextricably caught up in that knot

And node of myriad lives and issues met
In culmination in our latter day,
      When earth's wide stage was set
For cleansing retributions in the mortal play.

Therefore I see his life against a ground
Of battle, and he lies among the slain.
Again I hear the supernatural sound
Of guns on the horizon and again
Enter the belt of awe and zone of pain.

The frantic struggle to the table-land,
The ecstatic orgy of the battery's fire,
The pitch of expectation, the command,
The mad advance across the enemy's wire,
The giddy convoy as the foes retire.

Again I plumb that mystery of war
And in its depths discover all the past;
And there his figure rises up before
My eyes, a shade with countless shadows massed
In flight before the Winnower's viewless blast.

I see him in the feverish advance,
I see him in the battle's desperate throes,
Or lying prostrate in the ambulance
Where in the night war's black tornado grows,
Or sleeping in Romagne's endless rows.

His part was one with that prodigious myth
Of demi-gods, and now he slumbers with
The destined, summoned, unreturning sons
Of our revering commonwealth, the still
      The Silent Ones,

Caught up from our frustration to fulfil
A lot unprobed, portentous, and abide
Fixed in a shining splendor of noontide
        That never wanes,
Arrested in a glory that remains.

The Silent Ones that therefore live the more;
        By their Gethsemanes
Forever linked with heaven's sanctities
        And evermore
Omnipotent with ghostly armories
        To bring their will to pass,
Regnant above all infidelity.
        So they amass
Loyalties purified and such a freight
Of faith refined and an invisible weight
Of ardors and intentions that they see
Their deathless glory kindled in the obscure
And mediocre moments, and endure
And grow, and from their immemorial calms
Contagion flow and silently immure
In breathless climates of tranquillity
        Their grieved posterity,
Remote from trepidation and doubt's impious qualms.

February 1924

53

TO HENRY DE MONTHERLANT

On Re-reading "En mémoire d'un mort de dix-neuf ans," a chapter from La réleve du matin, *1918, in which the author raises a magnificent monument to his schoolmates lost in the war.*

WHO suffers and remembers?
 The fire has sunk to embers,
The echoes of your cry have died away.
And if the cicatrice
Some sudden day
Reopen, and the ancient pity burn,
When we, we too, return,
Who shall remember this?

Of that lost generation that now numbers
More of its members
In the eternal limbos than on earth,
You more than all in this our impious dearth
Have kept your fealty pure,
Have raised the elegiac strain and marked their sepulture.

They are not sensitive,
These throngs with whom we live;
No pities clutch them for our generation.
Those ill concealèd tears, that sweat like blood,
The accepted, ruthless, barbarous immolation,
They have not understood.

The world is gross:
What waste and lavishness of sacrifice,
And how ubiquitous a cross,
O how pathetic, how divine a loss,
Must be to thaw these senseless hearts of ice.

They fell like temples on the Acropolis
Of the ideal, yet who remembers this?

I swear, unless men take hold of this sign,
Their hopeless task the bleeding gods resign,
Abandon men to their lead-cloaked distress,
Their hooded pride, and pantherish loneliness.

They fell like statues, or as friezes fall
From temples in the hour of overthrow:
The band of marble topples from the wall;
Gods, Amazons and Titons sink below
The dust and terror, trampling and the foam
As of the steeds of Rome
When Pergamum saw all its glories overcome.

They fell like statues on the Delphic slope
Of dream and presage; who sustains their hope?

Who suffers and remembers
In these uncheered Novembers
The vernal travail that renewed the world?
Those throes are over, and those pennons furled.

"None are so dead as these,"
Their decent obsequies
By our conventional piety confirmed.
No seedling ever germed
From seed so deeply, brutally turned under,
Though sown in rain and thunder;
No Lazarus ever rose
From such unwept repose.

O tears of manhood issuing from the flames
Broken and stunned, O tears that scald and burn
Of outraged willingness that takes its turn
Yet once again with that which sears and maims;
Excess of bitterness, O tears of boys,
O smothered protests and despaired-of joys;

Say, in the tranquil other years beyond,
What peace and benediction, what surcease
Of pain, what suavity of love, what bond
Of quietness, and what release
Can ever compensate these tears of youth,
These tears of manhood? O exceeded hearts,
What amnesty can e'er assuage these smarts?
Since God's own life-blood flowed,
Since Christ His blood awoke our common ruth,
The human conscience bears no heavier load.

AS SHEEP WITHOUT A SHEPHERD

L INCOLN, compassionate surgeon of the throes
  Of anguish of two races, adequate heart
On whom the myriad hearts could lean their doubt,
Trembling at destiny's vast overthrows;

And Whitman, seer, who beneath the swart
Appalling storm, vermilion sky, walked out
In lightnings and the pandemoniac shows
Of hatred's discharge, and strife's dreadful rout,
To keep the marvellous vigil o'er the slain
And at the dawn with Christ's forefinger close,
And comrade-gentleness, the eyes of foes;
Seer by whose steps posterity doth gain
Access to the campaign, the rest, the assault,
And with whose eyes God pierced that night of pain;
In whom the epoch, as in light's default,
Saw itself and its hidden omens plain;

John Brown, thou rock of iron in the stream
Of man's facilities; obtrusive "nay"
Flung at the world's abandonments; thou "stay"
Out of the eternal, thrust up in the way
Of custom's, season's, time's complacent "yea";
Hallucination called, fanatic dream?
Nay, granite in the unsubstantial flux
Of shadowy wills whose futile torrent sucks
Toward nothingness, despite their seaming sway;

And Wilson, voice of the dead, "The President,"
Whose shattering challenge summed the dumb appeals
Of frustrate generations, as the peals
Of sharp, peremptory thunder give a vent
To gathered silences until earth reels:

Are then such overlords of time's events,
Such wielders of fate's arms and human powers,
Disposers of the conjunctures and the hours,
Redemption's hands and pity's instruments,
Are such withheld, and is man's virtue vain
Now when the hungering millions probe anew
The deep abysses of sincerity,
Nauseate with rank enslavements, and the few
Would see Christ formed within the race again
And timeless powers show in our mortality?

OLD AND NEW

ERINYES scourging half a world,
The nightmares of the East,
The condors of destruction met
At their unholy feast;
All this atoned for by the grace
That dawns in one unshadowed face.

I saw the flushed face of a child
Vibrant with laughter, half-upturned,
Eclipse a landscape red with strife
Whose copses smoked, whose hamlets burned,
And all that perished in that smoke
In those untainted eyes awoke.

I mourn no more the massacre,
I mourn less for the million dead,
The soil from which the poppy springs
With fabulous decay is fed,
And from the dark's engulfèd throng
Springs youth's immaculate new song.

THE EPIC PRESENT

No longer mourn the altars of the past
  And history's abandoned theaters,
Passion will still its noblest scenes outlast
And faith outlive its truest worshipers;
Nor mourn for some departed rhapsody,
Nor languish for the gray world's golden prime,
Not Marathon nor yet Thermopylae
Have been entangled in the mesh of time.
The Nikés, flying from Scamander's plain,
Late clapped their wings above our own advance,
Magnificence escapes from Caesar's train
To join our hosts on their triumphal way,
And from the crosses in the fields of France
Great tempests of redemption sweep, today.

ALMA MATER

S HE dwells in song, the mother of our hearts,
She dwells in silence and her cloister shades,
She dwells in memory, and her image starts
When all the present fades.

She dwells in echoes in the moonlit courts
By spectral tower flung athwart the stars,
And to the wards of reverie resorts
And draws the silver bars.

She dwells in memories of the patriot dead,
In poignancies that throng the haunted halls;
The tides that flooded round these walls and fled
Her vigilance recalls.

She dwells in music in the years to be:
I heard her chorals sweep from grander towers
Lifted on deeper hearts that spoke to me
Of more majestic hours.

O Mother, living in the hearts you breed,
Benign, whose gentleness hath made us great,
O Spirit of these precincts, Yale, O speed!
That vision consummate.

THE NEW APHRODITE

How art thou wooed, thou sister of the Fair,
  Thou other Aphrodite whom men ne'er
By Paphos or Valhalla's marble stair
    Looked on appalled?
    How art thou called?

Unborn! Unborn! Sister of Christ arise;
Start from the wave of Europe's tragedies
Or justify Iona's prophecies.
    Columba's isle
    Awaits thy smile.

Messiah-maid, messiah-mother, when,
When shalt thou bring thy gentler regimen,
And culminate Christ's kingdom among men,
    And mollify
    Our cruelty?

What drama of redemption is thy part?
What basenesses of ours shall break thy heart,
And which of our Sanhedrin cause thy smart?
    What Calvary
    Shall we pass by?

How art thou wooed? How shall we lead thee home?
Daughter of Thetis and the ocean foam;
Eve unbeguiled, sister of Adam, come!
    Our evil dream
    At length redeem!

NOTE. *There is an old Celtic prophecy to the effect that the Messiah will appear in the form of a woman at the island of Iona to usher in the Millennium.*

"AND WITH NO LANGUAGE BUT A CRY"

I HAVE a heart that cries to God
Abandonedly across the blind
Imperfect avenues of mind,
I have a heart that cries to God.

I have a heart that cries to God
Across the quarried stones of thought,
The labored temple slowly wrought,
A heart, a heart that cries to God.

I have a heart that cries to God
Immediately and must dispense
With faltering through the world of sense,
And calls across the mind to God;

That calls across the worlds to God,
Nor stays to elaborate the tongue
Of sacrament too slowly wrung,
I have a heart that cries to God.

DE PROFUNDIS

OUT of the utmost pitch of wilderment,
  Out of the stunned distress of ignorance,
Amazement, laceration, and despair,
The offering trampled, the derided ardor spent,
          Deliver us, O Lord,
And make thy power our truth, our sight thy Word.

From consternation's stroke, and the last hope
Bereft, and darkness' shattering scimitar
Counselling madness, and the palsied stand
Of those who in the noontide totter and grope,
          Deliver us, O Lord,
Fed from thy secret manna's hidden hoard.

From the blanched visage of affright, the soul
Smit with the rod of horror, tasting so
Creation's *culs de sac* of death, and black
Relapses of the species from the destined goal,
          Deliver us, O Lord,
And set our souls the effulgent issue toward.

From dreadful death, the wasting and the fire,
Corruption, and the obscenity of decay,
The torture of mad thoughts, and conscious course
Of soul-annihilation in sin's viewless pyre,
          Deliver us, O Lord,
With bread of health from life's abundant board.

"DALL' ORRIBIL PROCELLA IN DOLCE CALMA."—MICHEL ANGELO

I WOULD know mercy from the supernal calms;
I would know benediction and the balms
  Of the ultimate persuasions;
The unguents of the marble tomb, the night
Of death—its suavity and blest evasions,
The sudden space! the fragrance, and the starry flight.

There like some mariner from raging seas
And wastes chaotic past God's boundaries
Who issues on some halcyon reach, some floor
Of crystal, round a headland, while the roar
And carnival of storm behind him dies;

There in the elements' benign suspension,
There would I oar the breathless firmament
   In calm ascension,
   Released, unspent,
Trampling the aether with the eternal plumes
   Of exultation,
  Fanning those chambered glooms,
Lavender twilights, velvet far oblivions,
   With noiseless pinions
To some divined, remote angelic station.

INTERCESSION

Y E merciful angels! fend these quivering hearts,
And interpose, O God, thy merciful shield
For these exceeded souls.
Immure in heavenly safety, blessedly sealed
From bludgeon'd grief and all pain's furious darts
All thine o'erdriven souls.

Gather in providence about these heads
Sacred with pain, benignant ministers!
Hence and forever turn
In wreathes of calm where fiery gledes and cares
Revolved, and present stings and future dreads,
There ever wreathe and turn.

Enfold these spirits in love's ample skirt
Compassionate Christ! that stoop'st among the stars,
Environ them in thee;
Bereave of laceration, tears, and scars,
Nay, give thy glory and indue their hurt
With thine upon the Tree.

IN A HAMPSHIRE LANE

"He sendeth abroad his spirit
And the wilderness becometh a garden."

"He giveth to each a body as pleaseth him."

THE thoughts of God are flowers, not graven stones.
We read his scripture on the flaming slope.
We see him dreaming where the fragile cup
Of scarlet swells precarious by the lane,
Unfolded moist and glossy from the lap
Of being, still too sacrosanct for touch,
Swollen with the blood of God to affright the earth,
A new flesh broken from the brain of him.

The thoughts of God are flowers; and we are flowers
(Save for the worm), and trees are flowers, and groves
And earth and sea and sun and stars are flowers:
The thoughts of God unfolding in the light,
Waxy and delicate and fringed with dew,
Blown like a miracle from nowhere, swaying
Consistent and substantial, taken shape
And form and body from the invisible
In flesh of satin and incarnadine;
The thoughts of God congealed in space and time.

And earth and sea and sun and stars are flowers,
Corollas limpid, iridescent, woven
In timeless looms, a gelatine of light,
An ethereal vegetation from the unseen,
Sprung in a night; the thoughts of very God
Thus apparitional in imagery,
Like rainbows sprung from nothing. Earth and sea,

Clouds, and the silver fires of night and day,
All are but petals and the flesh of flowers,
All are but bodies of an intenser pulse,
More fearful touch, and a more thrilling clay,
Uprisen within the meadows of God's dream:
Gigantic bells of color, blinding sheets
Of textured flame, cohering films and webs
Of radiance: the systems and the suns.

And we are flowers, immaculate as they,
Kin to the azure and the dazzling cloud,
The billowing green; kin to the ecstatic lark,
Caught up to all the freedom of the fields
Of space and all the sanctities of light;
Divine and marvellous in flesh as they,
Coursed by their impulse, fired by the same flame,
Tongues from the identical hearth, and likewise swept
By the identical breath of exultation.
Our little gift of mind divides us none
From forms insensate and the instinctive world;
A candle to our needs, it adds no joy,
Else could we carol as the skylark pitched
Against the woofs of storm that drive aloft.
And we are fellow to the impassive height,
Kin to the veering birds, the irradiate copse,
The bronzed grain (deep within whose shimmering sea
The poppies flame out when the sun appears)
Kin to the careering cloud and cloudlike earth.

And man is as a vegetation, a tract
Of marvellous foliage washed and drenched in dew,
Sprung of the sacred earth and purified
By wave on wave of beauty, tides of color

That sweep the visible earth. For when the breath
Of God inbreathes the world, the wilderness
Of man becomes a garden tilled and rich:
He fills the world's face with his cities walled
With providence and paved with righteousness.
His towers show like flowerings of stone
And God's thought blooms in pigment and in clay;
And the still song within the heart of things
That shivers in the bosom of the cloud
And chants in swaying beeches at the dusk
Escapes anew in rhapsody and praise
Of mortal tongue and mortal instrument.

THE ARMORIES OF GRACE. *Cirque de Gavarnie*

"Hast thou entered into the treasures of the snow? or hast
thou seen the treasures of the hail,
Which I have reserved against the time of trouble, against
the day of battle and war?"—Job

I

HERE gaze and learn for once and for all time
To what effects of power grace hath recourse,
What arsenals of splendor to enforce
Capitulation and compel remorse,
            What arms of the sublime.
Here read compassion's limitless resource.
Here glimpse the reserves of God to win his race,
Marshaled upon these confines of the world,
His undeployèd ministries of grace,
            His glories furled,
            His cloakèd panoplies,
            Sequestered pageantries,
His shafts of dazzling lightnings all unhurled,
            The scimitars of beauty sheathed
            And javelins of radiance wreathed
            In leaden cloud,
Redemption's chivalry in flight on flight,
            With all their spears of light,
Dissembled in oblivion's mantling shroud.

Here read the measure of our impotence;
Standing aghast with wonder, augur thence
            The measure of our hurt
That to such rare anointing need resort.

Is then our dearth so great we need repair
To such a tabernacle, and so fair?
   How deep the wound must be
That calls for such surpassing ministry.
      How bounteous in resource
         Should prove the source
Of such persuasive medicines of ill,
Such balm for pain, such peace, such suavity,
Such sleep to breed, such heart's-ease to instil.

2

Beyond the Atlantian slopes whose reaches smolder
With burning bush in lavender and burnt gold,
As with quiescent flame; past bastioned shoulder
Upon whose charrèd pinnacles have rolled

The onslaughts of the gods; past canyoned gorges
Foaming with glacier streams whose freshets show
Like chrysoprase; and through the eternal forges
And chemistries of nature: ice and snow,

And warring elements and seasons' changes;
We mount into the parapets of the globe,
Toward strange domains and far-off lunar ranges
Wherein the steps of mankind rarely probe;

To issue on the pure haunts of God's mind
And tread the amphitheaters of snow
Set in the azure, whose white fires blind
The eyes of men with their cerulean glow.

The unsullied glories of the thought of heaven
Blazon untainted, and our eyes perceive
The divine imagination's reverie graven
Fresh from creation ere man's hand had leave

71

To smirch and smoke its splendors crystalline.
Around the circuit's Vulcan-forgèd sweep
Fences of granite run in terraced line
On line, and toppling on the remotest steep

See lodged aloft in angular lumbered heap
Cyclopian rocks that veer against the sky
(Around whose chalky eaves tornadoes sweep)
And pinnacles that float precariously.

3

Such are the gestures of the adamant
In the aerial fastnesses, and such
The dumb communications and the touch
Of the eternal in the soundless haunt
Of snow, that the superbest vaunt
Of hearts recalcitrant, and blasphemous
Offenses to the austerity of God,
Were here coerced to terror. Conquered thus
Impenitence must yield. The appalling rod
Of grandeur beats rebellion to its knees;
The intimidating whiteness of the peaks
Genders compunction; and the flashing streaks
Of hues unearthly racing on each slope—
Gestures of the divine indulgence
And mercy's unbelieved effulgence—
Would tame the fallen angels, and would cope
With the dark state of Judas, and must move
The Adversary himself to abjure harm,
Since Splendor of redemption is the arm,
And Beauty is the omnipotent sword of love.

CHRISTOS LOGOS

Δι' οὗ καὶ ἐποίησεν τοὺς αἰῶνας.

HEART of the world beyond the gleams of day,
O ardent sense, deep, deep in the life of things,
     Deeper than day and night,
Deeper than flesh and all time's shadowy rings,
Deeper than death, thou core of all, thou stay
     In the eternal night.

Thou corner-stone of the uranian nave,
Axis and center of wide being's girth,
     Thou polar star of souls;
O Cross pitched at the navel of the earth,
O spectacle this side, that side, the grave,
     O cynosure of souls!

O flaming heart from whom all kindlings start,
Impassioned dreamer of the universe
     Whose splendid impulse runs
In crimson floods of glory to immerse
And fill the ocean reaches of the heart
     Under its setting suns.

Spirit that moves in the unfathomed pit
Of thought, thou ghost in the aghast abyss,
     Haunter of mystery;
Conception darkens in us thence, and this
Thy mind is dark imagination's seat
     That broods on verity.

One life thou art in splendor and in love:
The face of nature takes its veil of dreams
From heaven's holiness;
An effluence of beauty sets and streams
Athwart the world from pity pierced above,
Whence every loveliness.

Through thee the worlds were made. It is enough:
One heart gives utterance in many forms;
Or in the firmaments,
Or in the face of man, or in the storms
Of earth's successions and the laws thereof,
Or reason's governments.

THE SON OF MAN

Thou child of man; thou birth of a travailing people;
Thou resurrection from a crucified race,
That through the blood and outrage and despair
Of faith's death-grip with flesh and circumstance
Conceived Thee in relapse on God and failure:
Ghost of expiring Israel in an hour
Estranged and alien: great Unrecognized,
Who brought with Thee to birth from Sheol's gates
Tending on Thee, millions of shadows strange,
Those who in martyrdom had fathered Thee,
Those who in suffering had dreamed of Thee,
From the intensest human had conceived Thee
Who most were Man, who most art Man today:
Who shall but verge upon the mystery
Of whence Thou drew'st thy oneness with all flesh?
Yet in the black night of the universe,
Yet in the blizzards of eternity,
The towers of men upon a thousand plains,
The swarming hordes in desert or by sea
Are but as cowering sheep, a single flock
Huddled in storm. The son of Israel
Is son of Man, for Israel itself
Was son of Man, Man's truest-hearted child
To affront the unknown and wrestle with the dark
And call up from the unimagined depths
Of desperation of the human heart
The indwelling Spirit to make answer there,
For, as the aghast tragedian cried out,
Though there be things stupendous, strange, divine
In multitude—yet none so much as Man.

Child of a race, and child of nature too
Whose bloody ascension finds its type in Thee:
O only drama true to reach on reach
Of human scrutiny and tragic record,
Thou only correspondent, truest norm,
Most central figure, representative.
Thy cross stands at the center of the world,
Thy moment summed the million destinies,
And *millions of strange shadows on Thee tend*
For Thou art heart of hearts, the substance self
Whereof we all are made in time and times.

And from the subterranean granite depths
Of man's existence, to this surface life
Of history which is of least import—
Phenomenal—Thou once did'st rise, here too
In this convulsive web of consciousness,
This shadow-strife and interplay of shades
Under revolving suns and moons, to make
Thy sign eternal in our temporal scene,
And in the landscape of our chained events
And time's successions (which are but a form
From nebula to nebula) and play
Of mundane fealties, to show Thyself
As Thou art in the timeless, once for all.

We saw Thee, O Thou Lover of Mankind,
Thy gesture in the daily dust of life
Was lovely, awful, and inevitable.
The total dark transaction of creation
From Alpha to Omega, dark to dark,
Was focused in Thy motions, entrances
And exits, in sublimest miniature.

We saw translated to earth's hieroglyphs,
And in the phantasies of human minds,
And in the imaginations of our kind
What veiled, inscrutable, unhuman fact
Underlies Being, and eternity.
For all the fulness of the godhead dwelt
In Thee, in our humanity's conceit,
And we have light hence evermore to walk
And scorn the dark between the stars, and blast
The sphinx with our eternal understanding.

ARACHNE

To Jules Deschamps

To Jules, a letter on the wings of song,
  A stratagem to foil the sorry wrong,
The grievous wrong of custom, and renew
The ancient lyric eagerness we knew.
Alas, the poverty, the drought of faith,
The penury of dreams, the failing breath
Of buoyancy and ardor in a life
Where only such supply endures the strife,
Where only such illusions stem the day,
Without whose gay battalions in the fray
We grope and stumble, and change worlds, to move
In darker phantasies where is no love.

Men live in their imaginings, and weave
Terrors and tempests round them or deceive
Their souls with self-wrought curtains of despair,
And caught in their dark folds they perish there.
Fabrics of every hue these spirits spin,
And every tissue, and then live therein,
And some there be like mansions wrought of flame
But most are webs of torment and of shame.

O to protest against the common sin
And weave a shrine all magical within,
So to escape the universal dearth
And be the Arachne of a fairer earth,
Fling out our iridescent filaments
And build our own unsullied firmaments.
'Tis but to nourish the precarious Fiction
Which is no fiction, with no dereliction;

'Tis but to feed the lie which is no lie,
Sustain the folly which is verity,
And walk the tight-rope of precarious faith
And keep alive the illusion unto death.
O 'tis a splendid rare insanity
And gallant make-believe, this poetry;
And then this faith, this Christianity,
What a divine impossibility!
To grasp the marvellous nonsense long enough
To bear undisillusioned earth's rebuff,
And create health from such sweet alienation
And healing from such rare hallucination.

Let us deny earth's truths and give the lie
Direct to all it swears and perjures by,
And mock the vain expediency that trusts
In artifice that fails and steel that rusts,
And gather round our souls the gossamer shrouds
And swathes of dreams like frail midsummer clouds
That form in heaven, and trust that in their hour
They too shall issue in effects of power,
Like clouds that in the still and sultry air
Gestate and charge themselves with portents there.
Learn from the storms that brood on breathless fields:
The soul's own heaven like surcharges yields,
Wrought out of reveries and dreams and prayer,
And as the lightning bursts above, so there
Eventual power shows itself, the dream
Takes act and shape to rock the things that seem.

Come, let us blind ourselves with high delusions
And lose ourselves in these most wise confusions

And let the world conserve its prudence! Come,
Indulge the sane, the sweet delirium.
Flee to the wildwood's heart, the wood of hope,
Plunge down the magic galleries and grope
Into its far lost precincts, well away
From cure and ransom to the glaring day.
Assert the claim to man's high-hearted quest,
Presume to share the eternity confessed
Nakedly on the common face of earth;
Thrill with the august throe of each day's birth,
And when the black leaves print themselves on dawn
Behold creation, leap the ages gone.

Plunge down the vein of romance; boldly steer
Onto illusion's shining hemisphere.
Drink at the far mirage, and take your bread
In passion for the morrow, and be fed
With wild adhesions to the causes lost,
And mad entreaties to the silent host,
The synod, the consistory of death,
Who must bestir themselves at mortal breath—
The imminent, the breathless throng that waits
In awe and power round the future's gates.
Wager your hearts *à l'outrance* 'gainst the world
And trust your protests up to heaven hurled.
Cut all the bridges of retreat behind
And win a world for ranging in the mind.
Remove to spheres that neighbor on those powers
Whose inclination can reverse these hours.
Acquaint you with the imagination's realm;
Ally you there with those that overwhelm
Markets and courts of law and masonry;
Anchor in the sure roads of phantasy.

Men live in their imaginings; so we
Shall occupy a web of glamory,
An iridescent fabric full of hues
To take the breath away: the royal blues
And purples of the humming bird; the stains
So full of dusk on medieval panes;
All rich and holy strainings of the light
Filtered through jewels to leave an irised night.
Such a hushed tabernacle love shall mold
And tenderness and pathos uncontrolled
Shall lend it depths of sanctity and awe
And wealth of intimation. Faith shall draw
Its soaring pinnacles high o'er the sod
In sweet presumption on the love of God.
And therein we shall live, and every grief
Shall turn to beauty like a fallen leaf
Alchemized into flame, and every care
Solvent in pity, ecstasy, and prayer.
There we shall live and out of such a cloud
Of dear intensities and ardors proud
Lightnings of prophecy and song shall strike,
To exonerate the dreamer and his like,
On listless earth, and thunderbolts of truth
To shock the world and flood the springs of ruth.

—Words! What shall words avail? The great cascade
Of instrumental voices that upbraid
The silence, and go plunging to the floor
Of being with their freight of human lore,
These carry our aspirings on their flood
But die. There is a summons in the blood
That knows no peace but action, and our fate
Alone the desperate urge can satiate.

Each in the eventual drama of his rôle
Shall find the true appeasement of the soul.—

Dreams are the wells of grace and through their deeps
Rise springs of life, and renovation sweeps
Upon the soul from opened gates of prayer,
Opened on the unknown. Man's birthright share
Of breath but hardly lasts the appointed length;
Nay death encroaches on him in his strength;
But new accessions of the essential life,
New increments of spirit, ease the strife
With the invading torpor, and we win
Draughts on the creative parenthood within
This zone of cold exhaustion and decay,
And heaven's soil feeds the ephemerae of earth's clay.

This moonlit midnight with its curded clouds
And jetty pyramids of foliage shrouds
Worlds of intelligences past our scope,
Alien economies. The teeming cope,
The living dome of light, pulsates and breathes
With undiscerned intensities and seethes
With "unknown modes of being" and unknown
Awarenesses and sympathies. Alone
Upon a shoreless sea of life and thought
I stand in stupor, impotent, untaught;
Marvel at the surpassing, strange eclipse
Of mortal sense. The holy fane outstrips
All mortal art. I dare not speculate
What tenderness, with what design elate,
What august life, or what serenity,
What cosmic gesture of deific glee,

Could fling that vault and overlay it so
With silver panels, and make darkness glow,
Silted with milky radiance, and sow stars
Beyond these leaves, beyond yon cloudy bars.
A god, a god makes sanctuary there
And with his motions is the night aware.

What shall the heart say when the heart is full,
Friend? How communicate the beautiful?
We know not what we feel, we only know
That round us silent tides do ebb and flow,
Mighty in impulse, from beyond the tomb,
That obscure apparitions fade, and loom.
What shall the heart say when the heart is full
And in what idiom or syllable?
Speech dissipates upon the hurricane
Of days and their wild passions. Song, again,
Dies, as the echoes of the reapers' strain
Grow faint along the burning slopes of grain.
The brimming Nile that in the expanded heart
Fills the horizon at the birth of art
In mighty onset under satellites
Of pale enchantment, soon resigns its rights;
In dreams alone the silver flood is rolled,
The inebriate fit is o'er, the heart is old,
The bronze is vacant and the marble cold.
The inner radiance that gave them glory
Withdrawn, the relics tell a soulless story.

Better to look into each other's eyes
Speechless, and read the language of surmise,
To clasp the hand and know that we are known,
Indeed persuaded we are not alone.

83

Better to write our legend in the mind
And memory of friendship, surely lined
By touch of human grace upon the wax
Of tenderness where fondness never lacks
The will to cherish or the power to hold
The character of thought inscribed in gold.
Better to laud God in the ear of love
Than carve Te Deums in the sacred grove.
Oh, let a thousand gestures feature me
In silent witness in your memory,
And sacraments of many an idle hour,
When words and converse languish, have their power
To breed the very converse of the soul
In all contempt of absence; though there roll
The breakers of far wider seas than these
Between, and dash on darker Hebrides
In stranger latitudes with hoarser chorus,
Beneath appalling nights and wild auroras.

Brussels, October 1924

L'ENVOI

THE pinnacles of dreams dissolve in sleep.
  The far-flung streamers of the soul on fire
        Smoke and expire.
The fabrics of the phantasy that leap
To crowd the vacant heavens of the mind
        Sink in the sullen deep.
The drowsed Arachne of the spirit fails;
        Oblivion veils
The webs of thought flung out upon the unconfined.

Shadows of God, we stretch us shadow lands;
We spin us ghostly firmaments of gauze
        With spirit hands.
Conception bodies forth a realm and draws
Its proper cosmos by its proper laws.

But darkness like a tide floods from beyond.
        The pitying wand
Of some reluctant Prospero compels
The erasing ocean with its solvent swells.
The half-formed palisades, the ribs of hills,
The dizzy platforms and the swaying towers,
Nebulous cities and their droning hours
        And rumored ills,
Reel to annihilation in the wrack
And dissipate to dust along old memory's track.

www.ingramcontent.com/pod-product-compliance
Lightning Source LLC
Chambersburg PA
CBHW071103090426
42737CB00013B/2445